The Family Legacy

Creating Generational Wealth . . .
Preparing for the Impending Crisis

LEONARD A. RENIER

Wealth & Wisdom, Inc.
www.wealthandwisdominc.com

ISBN 0-7414-2947-0

Published by:

INFINITY
PUBLISHING.COM

1094 New DeHaven Street, Suite 100
West Conshohocken, PA 19428-2713
Info@buybooksontheweb.com
www.buybooksontheweb.com
Toll-free (877) BUY BOOK
Local Phone (610) 941-9999
Fax (610) 941-9959

Printed in the United States of America

Printed on Recycled Paper

Published December 2005

ACKNOWLEDGMENTS

There are people who have influenced my life and my way of thinking, and who have helped me find the energy to write my opinions. My wife—Janice, whose love and support is the center of my life—gave me encouragement to complete this task. My children—Jacqui, Colleen, Beth, and Zeb—are with me every day in my heart and mind.

The people who expanded my knowledge in my business played an important role in my life. Don Blanton, founder of Money Trax, Inc., changed my career. His knowledge runs parallel with many of my thoughts. Much of my passion comes from the professionals across the country whom I've been fortunate to meet. They are committed and dedicated, and are a tremendous source of knowledge.

At the office, one of my associates, Grecia Souffront, played a major role and encouraged me to always "think bigger" when it came to this project. Nothing can replace the nice things she and all the other members of our office have done for me.

DISCLAIMER

This publication contains the opinions and ideas of its author and is designed to provide useful advice in regard to the subject matter covered. However, this publication is sold with the understanding that neither the author nor the publisher is engaged in rendering legal, accounting or other professional service. If legal advice or other expert assistance is required, the services of a competent professional person should be sought.

The author and publisher specifically disclaim any responsibility for liability, loss or risk, personal or otherwise, that is incurred as a consequence, directly or indirectly, of the use and/or application of any of the contents of this book. Any specific repetition in various published works from the publisher or others, unless noted, is an unintentional result of the nature of financial terminology and the fairly narrow focus of the financial writing and editing in which the publisher and author are involved.

Contents

Who Should Read This

Understanding that the family can be a very dynamic tool for creating generational wealth, this book was written simply to make more people aware of the possibilities and opportunities that lay hidden, yet are right before our eyes.

If you are a parent, grandparent or grown child of a strong, loving family, you should read this book. Although it is possible that every living generation of a family may prosper individually, it pales in comparison to the wealth that could be produced had they planned together as a single-family unit.

The techniques used to create this family wealth are simple, and based on logic. Dramatic demographic changes will place enormous demands on your financial future. Traditional thinking is not preparing you for these events. For the average American, it is time to enlist a new thought process.

The goal of this book is to create a defining moment in the way you think about money. That defining moment will occur with your understanding of the *Efficiency of Money*. The concepts that will be discussed are simple, yet effective methods of reducing and/or eliminating financial transfers of your wealth that you make every day, unknowingly and unnecessarily. Your savings, by utilizing some of these concepts, could be staggering. If properly suited, this knowledge could create more financial options and opportunities for you in the future.

The goal is also to help you through a thought process that will make you think a layer deeper when it comes to your money. Others are controlling your financial knowledge. They feed you enough knowledge to play the financial game but never enough to win. Financially, we are devoid of new ideas and have become brain-dead in our everyday financial dealings. We have become pallbearers for our money.

We have been defeated by banks, the government, taxation, credit card interest, automobile financing, mortgage companies, and personal debt. The evolution of transferring your wealth away to others is based on their ability to create situations, control the outcomes, and profit from it. Eliminating as many of these transfers as you can will change your life.

Everyone can profit from reading this book. It will be more effective for some than others. If you match up to just four of the nine following criteria, this book will change the way you think about money:

1) Strong household income
2) Owner of a home valued over $100,000
3) Married
4) Children
5) Participant in a retirement plan
6) Business owner
7) Executive, management-level professional

8) College educated and
9) 35 years of age or older.

If you have come close to matching four or more of these criteria, or will in the near future, you must read this book. When you do, you will be financially brought back to life. If you can accomplish this without spending one more dime than you are already spending, would you do it?

This book is NOT about helping you pick stocks or mutual funds or how to cheat on your taxes. It is NOT about offshore banking, financial pyramid schemes, or creating red flags for the IRS. It is NOT about clipping coupons, buying cheap products, or living on a minuscule budget. It is quite the opposite.

Knowledge is power. Knowledge can be time-consuming and expensive (the cost of this book). Now, consider the cost of not knowing something. There lieth the lesson.

Intent

The intent of this book is to introduce you to the idea of The Family Legacy, generational banking, and family wealth creation. The family remains one of the most powerful financial tools, yet is misunderstood and overlooked. It's time to take a fresh look at new ideas that will better prepare you for the uncertain future that we all face.

Today's News

NEWS FLASH

The Comptroller General of the United States was quoted in an AP interview: "I believe the country faces a critical crossroad and that the decisions that are made—or not made—within the next 10 years or so will have a profound effect on the future of our country, our children and our grandchildren. The problem gets bigger every day, and the tidal wave gets closer every day."[1]

NEWS FLASH

You owe $145,000.00! And your share of this debt continues to grow every day. Every man, woman and child owes this amount, just to cover all the promises the U. S. Government has made to creditors, retirees, veterans and the poor.[2]

NEWS FLASH

That $145,000.00 you owe does not include your personal debt such as mortgages, credit cards, car loans, college loans, etc. This also doesn't

---

[1] Tanner, Robert. "AP Poll, Analysis, Sound Alarm on National Debt," Associated Press, August 28, 2005.
[2] Hodges, Michael. "Grandfather Economic Report," http://mwhodges.home.att.net.

include the effect of increasing income taxes and property taxes. Also not included are the escalating costs of living that seem to increase daily. All of these increases have grown faster than our incomes.

NEWS FLASH

Government officials' and financial professionals' solution to these dilemmas is simple. You need to save more! How??? Indebtedness is swallowing America. According to the Bureau of Economic Analysis, saving as a percentage of disposable personal income is at its lowest rate since 1930, during the Great Depression.[3]

NEWS FLASH

Many believe they can make up ground via the stock market. That hope disappears on a daily basis. Some hope for inheritances, a windfall when their parents pass away. A very small number receive large estates. According to the Federal Reserve, of the 17% who received inheritances in the early 2000s, the average amount was $48,000.00.[4]

---

[3] http://www.bea.gov.
[4] Peterson, Peter G. Running on Empty. Picador. New York, 2004.

NEWS FLASH

It should be a surprise to no one that government agencies are projecting significant increases in future taxation. The idea of deferring taxes to a later date and a higher rate is not a good idea.

NEWS FLASH

Currently, the near future crisis is a four-headed monster that no one is attempting to slay. Right now, American Consumers are:

- Devoid of personal savings
- In credit card debt up to their eyeballs
- Working in a historic time where salaries are not keeping up with inflation and
- Mortgaged to the hilt on houses that are grossly overvalued.

On August 27, 2005, Alan Greenspan said the following: "Nearer term, the housing boom will inevitably simmer down. As a part of that process, house turnover will decline from currently historic levels, while home price increases will slow and prices could even decrease. As a consequence, home equity extraction will ease and with it some of the strength in personal consumption expenditures."[5]

---

[5]Remarks by Chairman Alan Greenspan at a Symposium sponsored by Federal Reserve Bank of Kansas City, Jackson Hole, Wyoming. August 27, 2005.

Rich People Think Like Rich People

Poor People Think Like Poor People

You Can't Be Aware Of Something You're Not Aware Of

Imagine all of the opportunities in life that you missed or that passed you by simply because you were not aware of them. I would like to discuss with you an opportunity that you may have that you're not aware of because no one has taken the time to discuss it with you. I believe that this opportunity could be so critical to your financial future that you should be made aware of the information, even if it is to say "no" to the opportunity. All too often, we are not exposed to situations that could really change our lives.

Limited Knowledge Equals Limited Choices

The vast majority of people are troubled and confused about the economy. They are bombarded by the media, bullied by sales people, and bewildered by the millions of things they need to know to survive in today's financial jungle.

Over the past several years, they have seen all the investment lessons they learned in the '80s and '90s, and even today, fail them. They know they can't live much longer on 4% and 5% rates of return; yet, they are scared and hesitant to make crucial decisions necessary to keep pace with the changing economic conditions. To make it worse, right now, 90 million Americans are faced with the most critical financial challenges of their lives.

I am going to shed some light on this darkness. I will break this problem down and analyze it carefully. Then, you will have a clearer view of choices that are available to you. You will feel more confident and prepared to make better financial decisions.

For years, planning professionals have operated under the theory that reducing retirement income and reducing the size of an estate reduced the taxation that one must face. The real concern should be centered on how to leave the most money and create the most wealth for your family or your favorite charities. If planning doesn't do this, what good is it? The goal should be to maximize your wealth with the least amount of money, and eliminate costs and taxes while securing the future for your heirs.

Can You Spare Some Change?

It is my observation that for the past 50 years the foundation of the financial services industry hasn't changed very much. I believe marketing and the media have made us more aware of financial products and services, and technology has made it easier to get involved, but the solutions have remained the same.

The average person is significantly limited in the options one can pursue financially. Traditional thinking can be broken down very easily: You can invest in the stock market; You can invest in real estate; You can invest in bank savings vehicles, and; You can invest in retirement plans. The one thing that remains constant with these planning options is that you, the consumer, are the only one at risk in these ventures.

Mr. Hyde, I Presume?

These types of investments come complete with dual personalities. Not only can you earn a few dollars, but they can also create a number of transfers of your wealth in the future. Traditional thinking could expose you to possible losses in the market. You could be charged fees for accounts, managers, and for maintenance, regardless of whether your accounts earn money or not. You may also have to pay income tax and capital gains tax, and there may be estate tax implications that you will face in the future. To summarize, over the past 50 years, very little has changed in the traditional approach to planning and its consequences.

The Undeniable Results

I have found, in my travels across the country, that many people have some things in common. According to the Federal Government, the average refund per taxpayer is about $3,000.00. This same typical American may have about $150,000.00 in their 401(k). The average person also owns a home. In that home, let's say this person has about $100,000.00 in equity. The average person may also have some other investments other than their 401(k). This would be mutual funds or stocks. Let's assume they have $20,000.00 in such accounts. It would not be uncommon for this person to have $10,000.00 in a bank savings account as well. So, the summary of this person's finances might look a little like the following.

$3,000.00	Annual tax refund
$150,000.00	401(k)
$100,000.00	Equity in home
$20,000.00	Investment funds (IF)
$10,000.00	Bank savings (BS)

All of this looks pretty normal for an average person. You might even say, that depending on this person's age, that they are doing pretty well. But let's take a deeper look at what is really happening here to the average American in this situation. Let's start with that average annual tax refund. What is the rate of return on that refund? The government has had your money all year; they must be crediting you interest for having the use of your money, right? Wrong! Your refund carries a zero percent rate of return on it.

Now let's take a look at this person's $150,000.00 in their 401(k). What would you say has been the average annual rate of return on this account over the past seven years? Remember, the events of September 11, 2001, may still have these accounts in negative numbers. But let's try to be positive and say this account has earned an average of 2% per year.

Let's now look at this person's $100,000.00 of equity they have in their home. Once again, what's the rate of return on this $100,000.00? It's zero percent. You see, the value of your home rises or falls regardless of how much equity you have in it.

As for this person's investment funds (IF) of $20,000.00, much like the returns in the 401(k), many of these accounts have had trouble getting back to the values they were at six or seven years ago. Let's just say this account also averages 2% per year. And then there is that fabulous bank savings account of $10,000.00. What's the typical rate of return on that money? One or two percent, if you're lucky, so let's just give it a 1.5% rate of return.

Now, let's summarize this person's accounts again. . .

$3,000.00	Annual tax refund	0% rate of return
$150,000.00	401(k)	2% rate of return
$100,000.00	Equity in home	0% rate of return
$20,000.00	Investment funds (IF)	2% rate of return
$10,000.00	Bank savings (BS)	1.5% rate of return

Take a step back and look at this for a second. How does it look now with the rates of return added in? Not all that terrific. Yet, we are not done. There is another issue we must address with these accounts, and it's called taxes.

Are there taxes on that annual tax refund of $3,000.00? In most cases, the answer is no. Will the 401(k) be taxed? Yes, when you start taking the money out of it. Is the equity in your home taxed? In most cases, under current law, the answer is no. Will the gains in that investment account (IF) be taxed? Of course, they will. Will the gains at the bank be taxed? Sure, they will. So now let's look at the same average person that just five minutes ago looked like they were doing pretty well.

$3,000.00	Annual tax refund	0% rate of return	Tax-free
$150,000.00	401(k)	2% rate of return	Taxable
$100,000.00	Equity in home	0% rate of return	Tax-free
$20,000.00	Investment funds (IF)	2% rate of return	Taxable
$10,000.00	Bank savings (BS)	1.5% rate of return	Taxable

Once again, take a step back and look at how this person is doing financially. Not only are the return rates not glamorous, but also when there is a rate of return, you get taxed on those gains. Remember, this is a typical scenario.

I would like to stop and say that we are finished with this person, but one more problem remains. Are there fees and charges attached to these assets? Unfortunately, the answer is yes. Is there a fee for the tax refund? Well, you may have had to hire an accountant to help you get your money back, and I would consider that a fee, so the answer is yes. Are there fees and management and expense charges in the 401(k)? Absolutely. Are there fees and service charges attached to your mortgage that includes the equity in your home?

The answer is yes. In a typical investment fund, are there fees, management, and trade charges? Yes. Are there fees in the bank accounts? Yes, yes, yes. So, let's summarize this one last time.

$3,000	Tax refund	0% return	Tax-free	Fees
$150,000	401(k)	2% return	Taxable	Fees
$100,000	Equity in home	0% return	Tax-free	Fees
$20,000	Investment funds (IF)	2% return	Taxable	Fees
$10,000	Bank savings (BS)	1.5% return	Taxable	Fees

I'm sorry, but no matter how I look at this, it doesn't look very good. What do you see? The funny thing is, for each of these accounts, the average person hired an expert to help them get these results. An accountant for the refund, a pension consultant for the 401(k), a mortgage broker for the home, an investment broker for the investment funds, and that "bank specialist" for the bank savings account. One way or another, you are paying these so-called experts. Five separate experts, not knowing exactly what's going on, doing, from what we can see in this example, a crummy job. The combined result of all this expert advice is financially killing the average American.

It is time to take a fresh approach to this problem. It's time to change the traditional thought process that got everyone into this mess in the first place. Giving you more knowledge to help you make better financial decisions in the future is the solution. This could change your life forever. The amazing thing is that you can do this without spending one more dime than you are already spending.

The Unavoidable Truth

To get a real grasp on what is occurring now and what is going to happen in the near future, we have to first come to one basic conclusion. Financial planning as it is being sold to the American public is not a science. After all, science is based on some certainties. If financial planning was a science, no one would have lost money. So don't get overwhelmed by all the hype that this is sophisticated science.

Let's imagine we could pile all of your wealth in the middle of a table. All the wealth you have, and even your ability to earn more money, is stacked up on this table. No matter how much money is there, everyone has something in common: They want their money to grow.

Traditional planning tells us that to make your wealth grow, you must invest in the right stocks and mutual funds. To increase your wealth, you must simply select the investments that will get you a higher rate of return. When investing to get a higher rate of return, who is the one at risk, you or the person making the recommendation? This is what we call a product solution. All you have to do is to buy the right investments at the right time, and then sell them when they reach their highest value, before everyone else does. The product solution has been the center point of traditional planning.

The problem is, it is difficult to get to the right solution when you start out with the wrong premise. Einstein once said, "You can't solve a problem using the same thought process that created the problem in the first place." The real challenge, financially, isn't what product will increase your wealth. The real issue confronting your future is the dramatically changing demographics.

Poverty Planning:
It Takes No Time
It Takes No Effort
Results Are Guaranteed

All too often, I see people doing the very basics, financially. With their heads buried in the sand, they take the ostrich approach to planning. The "wait and see" retirement strategy suits them well. Then, with limited or no financial knowledge, they attempt to survive in a world created for them by the government. They have been told that their pension and retirement savings will be enough to live on in their golden years. Let us not forget Social Security. But the ever-increasing cost of living, increasing taxation, and increasing cost of insurance drain the foundation of their future planning away. Often, they end up looking for part-time jobs after retirement. Pride, fear, and laziness fuel the ignorance of poverty planning. They receive financial advice from their friends and neighbors, but remain skeptical of anyone with professional knowledge. They work and work and never get ahead, and leave very little behind when they die. Unfortunately, they pass on the same financial lessons to their children as a legacy.

Financial Planning

As we established early on, the American public is bombarded by the media, bullied by sales people, and bewildered by the things it feels it needs to know. When it comes to finances, this is the confusion most people face. A lot of the conflict is created by several industries trying to profit under the guise of trying to help people financially. They provide products and/or services, both of which are for sale. Banks, investment firms, insurance companies, money managers, brokers, financial planners, lawyers, and accountants—all want your financial attention. All profess to have all the solutions to all your financial concerns. Who's right and who's wrong?

Most of these industries will try to convince you that the competition is inept, incompetent, and incomplete. The best defense is a good offense, and these industries are very busy trying to dismember their competition in front of potential clients. You can cut their arrogance with a knife. Don't get me wrong—there are a lot of highly skilled professional people out there, but they find it impossible to think beyond their own industry. A lot of their training and background will narrowly point their clients in one direction. If anyone suggests anything other than that one direction, they will be labeled as crazy. Thus, the confusion!

All of these industries are motivated by one thing—money. More specifically, YOUR MONEY! These industries make money via fees, commissions, and management and expense charges. They will always profess that "the other guy is ripping you off." It is disappointing and unprofessional that the people in this industry are willing to put the client (you) in the middle of these arguments.

You must find someone who knows and understands transfers of your wealth. If you don't, these groups will be simply asking you to give up some of your standard of living to fund their projects and programs. Without knowledge, you will remain bewildered.

Remember, these industries and salespeople believe that there is only one way to make your money grow: Through higher rates of return. Again, when chasing higher rates of return, who is the one at risk, you or the one making the recommendation? In a down market, who wins, you or them?

If you discover transfers of your wealth and reduce them, your wealth would grow, regardless of market performance. I call that growth *internal savings*. Let's take a look at some different types of planning and savings concepts available to the public, compared to internal savings.

INVESTMENT FUND [IF]

$80,000	Deposits
$6,000	Earnings
$4,800	Earnings After Taxes
Yes	Fees

BANK SAVINGS [BS]

$150,000	Deposits
$6,000	Earnings
$4,800	Earnings After Taxes
Yes	Fees

INTERNAL SAVINGS [IS]

$0	Deposits
$6,000	Earnings
$6,000	Earnings After Taxes
No	Fees

IF

In interviewing financial professionals, you are looking for someone who could best fulfill your financial needs. First, the investment fund (IF) salespeople say you could earn $6,000.00 in one of their accounts. You would have had to deposit $80,000.00 in the account. Unfortunately, you would have to pay capital gains tax on the growth and you would end up with net earnings of $4,800.00. There may also be advisory fees and account fees, based on your account balances and the type of account it is.

BS

Banks also want your business, so they introduce you to their bank savings (BS) programs. The bank says it too could get you a $6,000.00 return. All you would have to do is put $150,000.00 into their handy-dandy CD account. Of course, you would have to pay capital gains tax on your earnings, leaving you with $4,800.00. There may also be some fees charged annually to maintain this account, in addition to penalties if you want or need to withdraw some of that money before its maturity date.

IS

Now I come along and tell you about internal savings (IS) and teach you about transfers that you unknowingly and unnecessarily make every day. I say I can also get you a $6,000.00 return. The big difference is, you don't need to deposit any money in any account. Even more rewarding, there will be no tax on your gains and no fees or penalties involved. Finally, the coup de grâce: This is the only program where the $6,000.00 is guaranteed.

Now ask yourself: Do you want your financial future based on IF, BS, or something you know IS going to happen? Internal savings, by reducing transfers, also teaches the lessons needed to end the confusion that all the financial industries create. Remember, someone earning $75,000.00 a year, saving $5,000.00 of that income, would have $70,000.00 in residual income to pay all their bills and taxes. If you could internally save 1% of that $70,000.00, you would create a 14% rate of return on your $5,000 savings, with no market risk, fees, penalties, or spending one more dime out of your pocket. Does this sound like the type of financial advice and planning you would like to pursue?

In the comparison, you will notice that by utilizing internal savings and reducing transfers, you can increase your lifestyle and standard of living money. You may also be able to create your own "banks" and create more liquidity, use and control of your money, in addition to benefiting from significant tax savings. Converting transfers to internal savings will bring about that defining moment in the way you think about money.

As I stated previously, I don't believe in the way in which financial planning is being sold to the American public. There are good people out there to help you, but finding them is the trick. Measure them on their experience and knowledge. Make sure they surround themselves with other pro-fessionals and specialists, and, preferably, you were referred to them by someone you know and trust. Find someone who continues the process of teaching you the financial techniques you need to know and can use.

At War With The Future

Knowing what, and when, events are going to take place in the near future and how it will impact your life is essential. When it comes to your finances, having this type of information is critical. According to David Walker, Comptroller General of the General Accounting Office (GAO), to balance the budget by 2014, taxes on corporate and individual incomes would have to increase by 38%.[6] If taxes are not increased, then Social Security and Medicare would have to be cut by 55%.[7] The

---

[6]Walker, Hon. David M. *Truth and Transparency: The Federal Government's Financial Condition and Fiscal Outlook.* Journal of Accountancy, April 2004.
    [7]*Id.*

demographic shifts that ARE going to take place WILL deteriorate the situation even more. Walker states that if nothing is done by 2030, payroll taxes will have to increase by 100% and income taxes increased by 50%.[8] At that point, if taxes are not increased by those amounts, then Social Security, Medicare, and all non-defense spending would have to be cut in half. Quoting Walker, "Deficits do matter, especially if they are large, structural and recurring in nature. In addition, our projected budget deficits are not manageable without significant changes in the status quo programs, policies, processes and operations . . . We cannot simply grow our way out of this problem."[9]

The reason I point this out, is that the wisdom of saving money now and deferring the taxes on that money to a later date, may cause you great financial harm. If you have any plans of being financially successful in your later years, the taxation issue that will be waiting for you will not be a friendly one. The hopes of saving taxes by using government-sponsored qualified plans (IRAs, 401(k)s, SEPs, etc.) are diminishing by the second as the demographics change and the government continues to spend $1.58 for every dollar it takes in. The U.S. Treasury Financial Report stated that in the fiscal year 2004 the spending shortages in Social Security and Medicare were eight times the total amount of government spending in fiscal year

---

[8] *Id.*
[9] *Id.*

2002.[10] That comes to about $200,000.00 for every household in the United States. That amount of money is about double the value of all the stocks, bonds, and mutual funds that all Americans now own. To make things worse, the Congressional Budget Office states that the assets of the Social Security Trust fund do not represent any real stock of resources set aside to pay for benefits in the future.[11]

The taxes collected from you and I for Social Security and Medicare are deposited into the government's general fund and spent immediately. The Social Security and Medicare fund are credited with an IOU, to be paid back at a later date. Some of the people who will have to repay this huge debt have not yet been born.

Doom and Doomer

It is my opinion that the public is not well informed of these issues. It is almost like the financial services industry and the government believe the public doesn't really need to have this information. But having this information and realizing how it will impact your financial future is critical to preparing you for that future. Many professionals and people in government would have you believe that you are too dumb to understand the

[10]http://www.fms.treas.gov/fr
[11]http://www.cbo.gov

total picture of the future. These people have plans for you; their plans are not yours. Their plan is the evolution of transferring wealth away to those who create the situations, control the outcomes, and profit from it. You see, information is on a need-to-know basis when it comes to their plans. These so-called experts have determined that you don't need to know. Without knowledge, the future will be filled with unintended consequences.

The Government's Role

Several years ago, I realized that the public's general attitude toward government fiscal responsibility and traditional personal financial planning was one of mistrust. This was solidified with the aftereffects of 9-11 and the fall of the stock market. There was very little knowledge being passed around. Even prior to the terrorist attacks, the public was not being educated enough to make good personal financial decisions. Very few Americans can even tell you what tax bracket they are in, how much is in their retirement plans, or where it's invested. But all of our financial futures will be centered on the actions or inactions of the Federal Government.

I knew that my mission—to educate the public on these issues—would be met with some criticism. But the earth is not flat. I found there is a lot of support and agreement about the direction in which we are headed and how it will impact all of us. The media, who normally loves a great disaster, is politically ignoring the obvious warning signs. The following are some official comments from government agencies that are NOT making front-page news.

"The Social Security and Medicare shortfalls compel change. They must not be left hanging over the heads of our children and grandchildren. The longer the delay in enacting reforms, the greater the danger, and the more drastic the remedies will have to be."[12]

"Without changes to federal programs for the elderly, the aging of the baby-boom generation will cause a historic shift in the U.S. fiscal position in coming decades . . . Federal spending on the major health and retirement programs—Social Security, Medicare, and Medicaid—is projected to grow by more than two-thirds as a share of the economy by 2030 . . . Consequently, either taxes will need to rise dramatically, spending on other federal programs will have to be cut severely, or federal borrowing will soar."[13]

"The fundamentals of the financial status of Social Security and Medicare remain highly problematic. Although both programs are

---

[12] U.S. Office of Management and Budget, *President's Budget for Fiscal Year 2004* (2003).
[13] Congressional Budget Office, *The Budget and Economic Outlook: An Update* (2003).

currently running annual surpluses, these will give way to rapidly rising annual deficits soon after the baby boom generation begins to retire in about 2010. The growing deficits will lead to rapidly mounting pressures on the federal budget in a decade and exhaustion of trust funds in little more than two decades that will not permit payment of currently scheduled benefits. In the long run, these deficits are projected to grow at unsustainable rates."[14]

"The current system is financially unsustainable. Without reform, the promise of Social Security to future retirees cannot be met without eventual resort to benefit cuts, tax increases, or massive borrowing. The time to act is now."[15]

"In 2008—just four years from now—the first cohort of the baby-boom generation will reach 62, the earliest age at which Social Security retirement benefits may be claimed and the age at which about half of prospective beneficiaries choose to retire; in 2011, these individuals will reach 65 and thus will be eligible for Medicare. At that time, under the intermediate assumptions of the OASDI trustees, there will still be more than three covered workers for each OASDI beneficiary; by 2025, this ratio is projected to be down

[14]Social Security and Medicare Board of Trustees, *Status of the Social Security and Medicare Programs: Summary of the 2003 Annual Reports.*

[15]President's Commission to Strengthen Social Security, *Interim Report* (2001).

to 2¼. This dramatic demographic change is certain to place enormous demands on our nation's resources—demands we will almost surely be unable to meet unless action is taken. For a variety of reasons, that action is better taken as soon as possible. "[16]

"These long-run budget projections show clearly that the budget is on an unsustainable path . . . As the baby-boomers reach retirement age in large numbers, the deficit is projected to rise steadily as a share of GDP. Under most scenarios, well before the end of the projection period for this chapter rising deficits would drive debt to levels several times the size of GDP." [17]

"If you look ahead in the federal budget, the combined Social Security or OASDI program together with the rapidly growing health programs (Medicare and Medicaid) will dominate the federal government's future fiscal outlook . . . Absent reform, the nation will ultimately have to choose between persistent, escalating budget deficits, significant tax increases, and/or dramatic budget cuts . . . Taken together, Social Security, Medicare, and Medicaid represent an unsustainable burden on future generations." [18]

---

[16]Federal Reserve Board Chairman Alan Greenspan, *Testimony to U.S. Congress* (2004).

[17]U.S. Office of Management and Budget, *Analytical Perspectives on the Budget* (2003).

[18]Comptroller General of the United States, *Statement to the Special Committee on Aging of the U.S. Senate* (2003).

Tax hikes of record proportion will be needed to keep government programs and benefits going. It is logical to believe that our children will pay even more taxes and receive fewer benefits than we will. A male who retired in 1965, who received a lifetime of Social Security benefits, would have received an 8.5% rate of return on the taxes he paid to get those benefits. A male retiring in the year 2000 would realize a 1.6% rate of return, and in 2030, it will be down to a 1% rate of return on the taxes paid for those benefits.

The Next 20 Minutes Could Change Your Life

I have had the opportunity on a few occasions to speak at the Federal Reserve of Chicago's Money Smart Week. To my surprise, a segment of my speech received the highest reviews, and was subsequently aired on local television stations. I was humbled by the praise I received, but more important than that was the message that was delivered, and the public's response to it. Remember, you can't be aware of something that you're not aware of. With that thought in mind, I would like to share with you a thought and an idea that could change your life forever.

The
Family
Legacy

The Vanishing Legacy

With the final breath, it all ended. All the lifelong dreams, the fifty years of work, raising a family, the pain of losses, the memory of joys and happiness—gone. Now all that is left of that life are the memories of that person and the legacy of a lifetime. To those left behind, the memories are theirs to keep, but everything else must be divided into two categories: what they are allowed to keep and what the government claims belongs to them. What is truly unfortunate is that the government claims must be settled first, and what is left is divided between creditors of the deceased and members of the family.

A hundred years ago, it was not uncommon for farms to be worked and owned by a family. The grandparents were there working and contributing to the farm, along with their middle-aged children and their grandchildren. The family structure was whole. Family pride was evident, and this was passed on generationally. The older members of the family were well aware of the idea of legacy. They worked hard to create a better life for the next generation. The farm, along with the memories, was their legacy.

Today, that element of a family legacy has almost disappeared. Although there are loving memories, the passing of the family "farm," today known as family wealth, has been mismanaged into non-existence. Interference from the government, an enormous lack of financial knowledge, along with pride and ignorance—all rob families from passing tremendous amounts of wealth to the next generation. Along with it goes the lasting family legacy.

When no one pays attention to the everyday details of the farm, it will no longer be a productive entity to pass on, and in many cases, it will become a burden and a debt to the next generation of the family. Today, the idea of viewing the family as a single unit has been ignored by almost everyone; yet, it remains as one of the only solutions for creating lasting family wealth, generationally. The passing of the family wealth (the farm) doesn't occur accidentally. It is planned and well thought-out. Rich people do this often, and their families remain rich. Poorer families, although their lives may prosper, believe in taking it with them when they die. Their legacy is usually a home, some savings, and other (for lack of a better word) stuff. Although those things have value, they pale in comparison to what could have been passed on had the entire family planned the family legacy seriously.

The idea of keeping wealth in the family is opposed vigorously by the government because they have a harder time getting their hands on this money via taxes. Many politicians try to pit the rich against the middle class, all the while the middle class aspires to be rich, pursuing their financial dreams via the lotto and casinos. The difference comes down to this: Some families guarantee their ongoing legacy, while others gamble it away.

The Social Fiber of The Country

The United States started to lose an important social foundation in the 1960s. Crisis after crisis, from Vietnam to civil rights, the drug culture to presidential assassinations, the once starry-eyed nation woke up with a reality hangover that would plague it forever. What would suffer the most in this historic time would be the family structure. The "what's in it for me" and the "I want it now" generation blossomed and grew up to train and educate the next generation, flaunting the wisdom of ME and I.

The family social structure, once the cornerstone of ethics and morality, started to crumble, and with it, family opportunities also crumbled. The growth of single-parent families left little room for financial success. Government social engineering only created more problems and greater dependence for its so-called "free" benefits. That dependency aided the problem, not the solution. The aftereffects of the loss of the family structure continue to cost the government billions of dollars. Along with the costs are increasing crime rates, suicide rates, divorce rates, and personal debt and bankruptcy rates. All of these have a direct correlation to the loss of the family structure.

Institutionalizing Educational Standards

With the fall of the family structure, the liberalizing of education took on the role of psychologist in making kids feel okay and being sensitive to their every need. The new educational goal was that no one would fail in school. They would only fail after they were out of school. The ability to apply school knowledge to everyday circumstances is non-existent. Not only is the knowledge missing to grow wealth, but also missing is the family and its ability to grow wealth generationally. In the old days, this would be the equivalent to the grandparents leaving the farm before they taught their kids the farming process. Obviously, nothing would grow, which is why in today's family, nothing is growing either. More time and energy are spent on teaching you how to spend your money, rather than how to save it. You end up unknowingly and unnecessarily giving away your wealth and wealth opportunities.

If tomorrow you discovered an opportunity that, by planning together with your parents or your kids, could create millions of dollars for your family (or charities), would you take advantage of that opportunity? If you also discovered that the money could be transferred to your family, guaranteed and tax-free, would you do it? I have reason to believe that you were not taught how to do this in school, any school.

Creating The Legacy

It came to my attention while visiting the San Diego Zoo that every animal display had something in common. Each one of them was funded or sponsored by a family or family foundation, AKA generational family wealth. The question that came to my mind was: What did these families do, that others didn't or don't do? The revelation hit me like a ton of bricks: They leverage the least amount of money to create the most amount of wealth by investing in their family. The rich follow three basic rules to accomplish this.

RULE NUMBER ONE: In your family, use the least amount of money to create the greatest amount of wealth.

RULE NUMBER TWO: Guarantee that the wealth will occur and the legacy will transfer, tax-free.

RULE NUMBER THREE: Create multiples of wealth immediately.

That was the answer. It was clear, and believe me, it was the best trip to the zoo I ever experienced. On the way home, though, one thought kept echoing through my head: Rich people think like rich people; poor people think like poor people. It was troubling. I asked myself one question: Would someone want to create wealth for their family if they didn't have to spend one more dime than they were spending right now? If you could realign your assets to make wealth possible, and still retain control of the money, would you do it? The key to all of this is to consider the family as an investment.

Controlling The Asset

Investing is not about where your money is, it's about how you can use it to create wealth. This is far different than buying a stock and praying that the stock will go up. Warren Buffett never buys 100 shares and just holds them. He, like Mark Cuban, buys shares of a stock to get some level of CONTROL of the company. If you have the resources to take control of a company, and you think it's a great investment, do it. If you want to try to guess on a company, buy their stock, and hope it goes up, you might as well go to Las Vegas, because you have no advantage at all to CONTROL the value of that stock.

In the old days, the family had total

CONTROL of the farm. The family could affect the growth and outcome of the farm they owned and CONTROLLED. Today, in generating family wealth, dabbling in stocks and mutual funds doesn't provide the ownership and control that is needed to pass on wealth successfully. The elements that affect these types of legacies are taxes, risk, creditors, and luck. In defense of many who follow this strategy, professional advice has told them this is the only way to create wealth.

Leverage

Unfortunately, following traditional investment plans does not create multiples of wealth immediately. If a family asset is not being used to generate income, then that asset should be used to create family generational wealth. You would want to insure and guarantee that the wealth be transferred to the family, tax-free. Most importantly, you would want to expend the least amount of money to create the most wealth. This is known as *leverage*.

The Contract

If you were able to invest in an older member of your family and he/she allowed you to do so to create the ultimate family legacy, what investment would be used? Life insurance. It is the perfect solution for family wealth creation. It is a contract the family CONTROLS. The cash value and death benefit grow, tax-deferred and tax-free. It is protected from creditors and passes outside of probate. Any number of family members, including the parents, can contribute to the premiums. This creates the greatest family legacy that will pass on to the family, using the least amount of money. All of this is centered on the legacy of love. This will be a very emotional decision and should be viewed with the proper perspective. In the old days, all members of the family would invest all their time and money to increase the wealth of the farm, knowing some day it would be theirs. They didn't do this out of greed, but out of love for the family.

To Whom It May Concern

I would like to address this issue of The Family Legacy on two different levels—the older crowd (you know who you are) and their children, who are probably 30 years old or older.

Lifelong Dreams

I was speaking to an elderly group of people, and I asked them a very direct question: "How many dreams and goals, that you had when you were 20 years old, actually came to be in your life?" The room was quiet. Many felt fortunate to be there. They had seen the wicked turns that life can take and the stings of disappointment. But they did have one thing in common: They all wished things could have been a little bit better.

"Everyone here probably got married and started thinking about raising a family. Children were born, and reality set in. It is very expensive to raise kids. Some of the initial dreams you had when you got married had to be set aside. The idea of providing for your kids became first and foremost. You wanted to provide a better life for your children, even at the sacrifice of your dreams.

"Your kids grew up, went to college and moved on, and you realized you had to start saving for your own retirement. Once again, dreams and goals were set aside to avoid the crisis of not having enough money at retirement. You saved and saved, with what seemed like very little progress, while giving up the things you really wanted in life.

"Retirement comes. You've made it. The lifestyle you have been accustomed to may have had to change somewhat, but you're okay. You have time to reflect back on your lives and wonder: What would have happened if you had been able to fulfill your dreams? Would your entire family have benefited from your success? And would these dreams have created a legacy to give to your family?

"Today, if you had the magic to recapture all the dreams and goals that you had during your lifetime and give them to your children and grandchildren without spending one more dime than you are already spending, would you do it? It is possible that the opportunity is right before you today, but you are simply not aware of it."

Opportunity of My Lifetime

I would like to share with you an example of how The Family Legacy can dramatically impact your life. First of all, you have to make your family aware that this opportunity exists, as I did with my family. I held a family meeting to discuss the situation.

I told my family that I was deeply concerned about the path that we are headed as a country and a society. I told them that I was fearful of the changes that would affect their lives and the impact it would have on their ability to survive financially, in the future. I asked them that if they had an opportunity to prepare for this uncertain future without spending one more dime than they were already spending, would they do it? I looked at them and said, "The opportunity to do this is right in front of you sitting at this table."

You see, I wanted to give my family an opportunity of a lifetime. I wanted to create a family legacy that would be the foundation for not only their financial future but also for their children, my grandchildren. I realized that my children now had their own families, and their ability to build real lasting wealth was limited. I told them that I knew their future would be challenged by fluctuations in the investment markets, and the future tax increases were a certainty due to the tremendous changes in the demographics in the near future. In my discussion with them, I wanted them to seek out every opportunity that we had as a family to create real wealth. The goal was to spend the least amount of money to create the most amount of tax-free wealth without any additional money being spent.

I took a second and told them: Rich people think like rich people; poor people think like poor people. The difference between the two is that most rich people insure and guarantee that their wealth will be passed on to their families, tax-free. Well, the real truth is that most of us are not rich. I said, "I would also like to pass on as much wealth to you as I possibly can. I would like to use my life to maximize the amount of money that I can offer you." It was quiet at the table, and I said, "The opportunity to accomplish this is sitting right in front of you. I want to offer you the opportunity to invest in me. I want to do this out of love, as a family legacy for you and my grandchildren."

The Legacy Opportunity

The obvious response from everyone, including my family, is: How do we do this? Well, there are really a lot of ways to create a family legacy. People simply are not aware of them. You see, you cannot be aware of something that you're not aware of. An example of one of the ways I could create a legacy for my family could be presented as follows.

Creating the legacy I discussed with my family would not involve one dime of my money, nor would any members of my family spend any more money than they are already spending. This would be their investment in me. We needed a vehicle that gave them tremendous financial rewards, utilized the least amount of their money, and would pass the money to them tax-free. As rich people do, we insured and guaranteed that these things would occur. They purchased a life insurance contract on me with the highest paying death benefit, using the least amount of premium they could to fund it. To pay for this, they stopped over-funding their 401(k)s and outside investments, and stopped making any additional payments to mortgage principal. Between them, this came to a nice sum of money. My kids are in their early 30s. If I lived another 10 years, and the death benefit came due (i.e., I died), the internal rate of return on their investment in me would be about 36% tax-free. If I lived another 20 years, instead of 10 years, the internal rate of return would be 13% tax-free. Even at the age of 80, the internal rate of return would be about 10%, and would create about $1.7 million dollars for them tax-free, upon my death. My kids would own the policy and have access to the values in it, even while I was alive. It is also possible for me to contribute additional money to this contract to increase the amount of the legacy to my family.

IMPORTANT NOTICE

The example above is just an example, and the numbers used are only estimations and will be different for everyone. Premiums differ from company to company. Age, health, and insurability will affect premiums. To see if you qualify and to get internal rates of return, contact an experienced, licensed professional.

My example was meant to be simplistic in nature, yet create dramatic results. There are many ways, in a family setting, to create and fund a Family Legacy, and at the same time, reduce future taxation. It also addresses the issues of a financial future that is filled with uncertainty. This is not a trendy solution that fades as markets change; rather, it is a solid foundation for creating wealth in the future. The legacy increases the family's money supply now and in the future. It creates more and better benefits for you and your family. The legacy reduces the amount of risk and future taxation that you would typically be exposed to. It is also possible that all of this can be achieved without spending one more dime than you're already spending.

Knowing what is going to happen in the near future can give you a distinct advantage in preparing for the challenge ahead. The sudden impact of the demographic changes will affect everyone. Higher taxes and one's ability to save are major concerns in the future. Imagine the idea of creating future wealth in a family and having it pass tax-free. Now imagine waking up tomorrow knowing that your future was financially secure. How would your life change? All of this can happen if you understand a few simple lessons—Leverage use; Asset control; Debt as a financial tool; Liquidity, use and control of your money; and Lost opportunity costs. These lessons will help you reduce the transfers of your wealth that are occurring every day, unknowingly and unnecessarily. Recapturing these transfers could help you create a family legacy.

Rich people think like rich people; poor people think like poor people. Once again, the difference between the two is rich people know how to secure their wealth for the next generation. First, they know how to use the least amount of money to create the most amount of wealth. Second, the rich guarantee that the wealth will occur and that the legacy will transfer tax-free. Finally, they create multiples of wealth in the legacy immediately. This is exactly what I did in my example with my family. I did this for my family to give them at least a fighting chance to survive in a future that was laid out previously in this book. Is the family legacy the solution to all the future problems? No, but it's a powerful tool for building a secure future for the ones you love.

Why I Did This

It is my concern that the path we are on financially, both personally and as a country, will have an impact on everyone. This book was meant to make you aware of something that you possibly were not aware of. The challenges we will be forced to confront due to the dramatically changing demographics, and the course that has been set by the politicians we elected, will financially be overwhelming. Unfortunately, as a society, we may drown in debt. People who now realize the problems that are coming can now focus on solutions and get prepared. The book was also meant to introduce you to ideas and opportunities that will help guide you through this uncertain future. This book was meant to create questions in your mind, so you can have a serious discussion with a professional who has been trained to give you educated answers. Everyone's situation, opportunities, and solutions will be different.

With all the perils that are confronting you in the future, you owe it to yourself and your family to consider The Family Legacy.